REUSABLE ROCKETS

and Other Space Tech

World Book, Inc.
180 North LaSalle Street
Suite 900
Chicago, Illinois 60601
USA

For information about other "Cool Tech" titles, as well as other World Book print and digital publications, please go to www.worldbook.com.

For information about other World Book publications, call 1-800-WORLDBK (967-5325).

For information about sales to schools and libraries, call 1-800-975-3250 (United States) or 1-800-837-5365 (Canada).

Library of Congress Cataloging-in-Publication Data for this volume has been applied for.

Cool Tech
ISBN: 978-0-7166-2429-5 (set, hc.)

Reusable Rockets and Other Space Tech
ISBN: 978-0-7166-2436-3 (hc.)

Also available as:
ISBN: 978-0-7166-2453-0 (e-book)

2nd printing November 2021

STAFF

Editorial

Writer
  William D. Adams

Manager, New Content
  Jeff De La Rosa

Manager, New Product
  Development
  Nick Kilzer

Proofreader
  Nathalie Strassheim

Manager, Contracts and
  Compliance
  (Rights and Permissions)
  Loranne K. Shields

Manager, Indexing Services
  David Pofelski

Digital

Director, Digital Product
  Development
  Erika Meller

Digital Product Manager
  Jonathan Wills

Graphics and Design

Senior Designer
  Don DiSante

Media Editor
  Rosalia Bledsoe

Manufacturing/
Production

Manufacturing Manager
  Anne Fritzinger

Production Specialist
  Curley Hunter

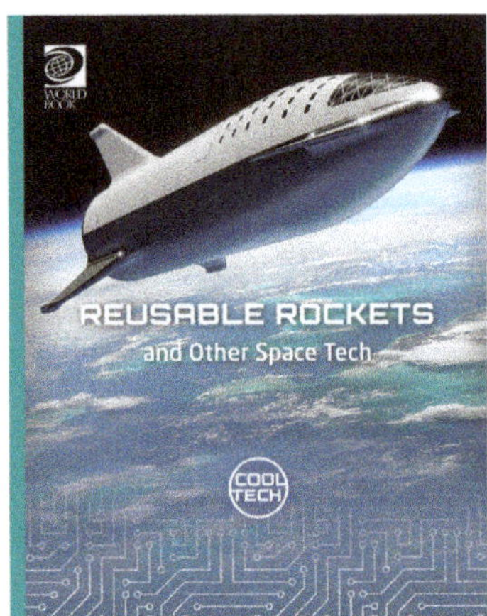

Credit: SpaceX

CONTENTS

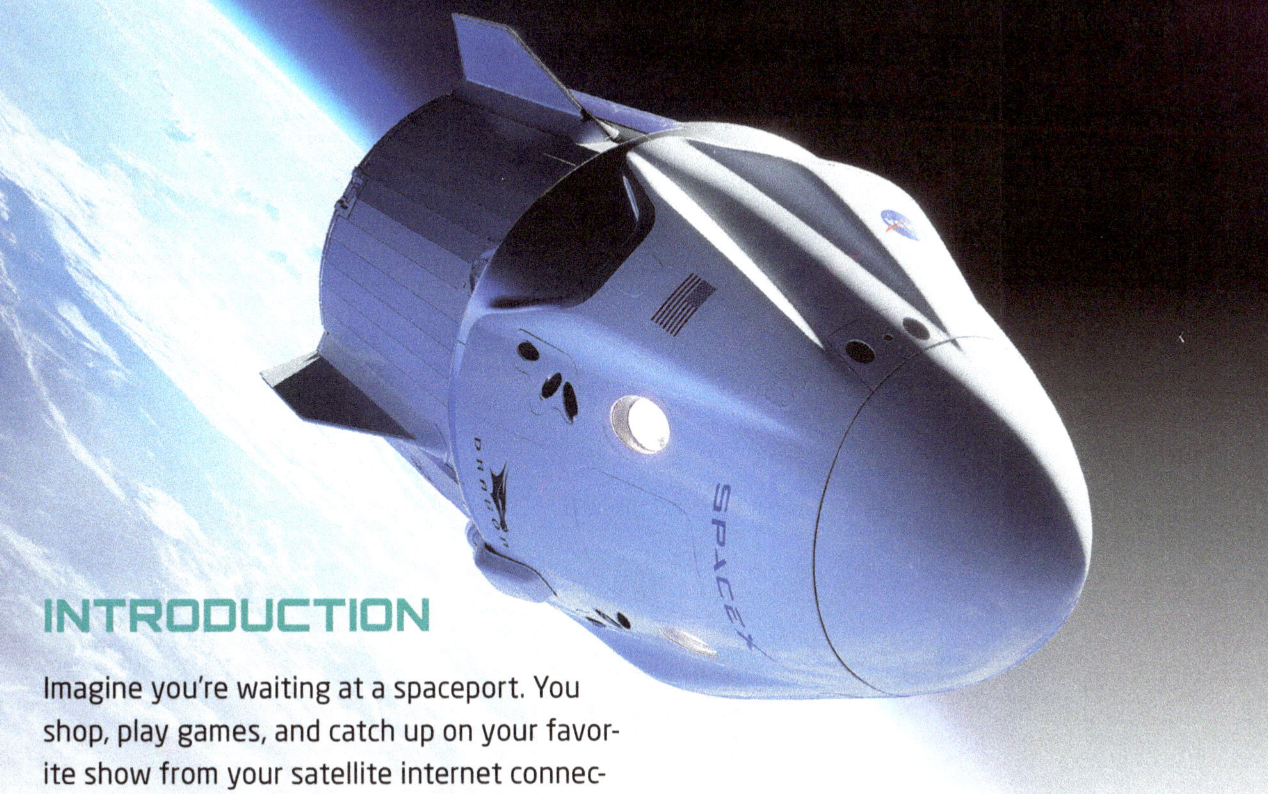

INTRODUCTION

Imagine you're waiting at a spaceport. You shop, play games, and catch up on your favorite show from your satellite internet connection. You board a sleek spaceplane which takes off and climbs into the sky. After an hour of flying you're weightless—but you don't bother to unbuckle from your seat to experience it. You're heading to a huge **orbiting** space hotel, where you'll enjoy a week of stunning sunrises, stargazing, and weightless sports. There will be plenty of time for graceful pirouettes in your own private room!

Space is only about 60 miles (100 kilometers) above our heads. But in many ways, it feels farther away than that. Humans last set foot on the moon some 50 years ago. The iconic United States National Aeronautics and Space Administration (NASA) space shuttle has been retired for a decade. All the planets in our Solar System have been explored. Knowledge of the cosmos is great, but aside from that and some cool pictures, what has space done for you? And what can it do for you in the future—and when will that future get here?

You or people you know probably use space technology every day, even though you might not realize it. Your smartphone navigation system, satellite television (of course), and even credit card payments all use satellites. In addition, the exploration of space has propelled development of technologies that many of us use all the time, such as Velcro, memory foam, and cordless drills.

It's been a long time coming, but soon space technology may do even more for you than it does right now. Today, new developments are bringing space closer to us than it ever has been before. Reusable technology is making it cheaper, safer, and easier to get to space, creating opportunities for new science, products, and services. Someday soon, people will visit space for business and pleasure, finally fulfilling the promise of the Space Age. Maybe you'll go someday!

REDUCE, REUSE, SAVE MONEY

Imagine that when an airplane reached its destination, everyone parachuted out of the plane with all their luggage and the plane was remotely flown away to crash into the sea. How wasteful would that be! Air travel would be exceedingly rare and expensive.

The fact is, most spaceflight is conducted in this way today. Multimillion-dollar rockets propel astronauts, satellites, and supplies into orbit and are promptly jettisoned to smash into the nearest ocean or burn up in the **atmosphere.** This wastefulness is one of the reasons spaceflight is so expensive. If even some parts of a rocket could be reused just a few times without the need for major maintenance or repair, it could drastically bring down the cost of getting things into orbit.

This is exactly what engineers are doing today. Led by the American company SpaceX, governments and private companies are getting used to the idea of rocket reuse. They are breaking down the barriers to space access.

THE SPACE SHUTTLE SOARS, BUT REUSE FALLS FLAT

Reusing rockets is not a novel concept. Once people began going to space, **engineers** came up with ideas for reusing parts of spacecraft. The first attempt at a reusable spacecraft was the space shuttle, developed by the United States National Aeronautics and Space Administration (NASA).

Compared to other rocket designs, the space shuttle looked bizarre. A large spaceplane, called the orbiter, was strapped to a colossal tank of fuel for its engines. On the sides of the fuel tank were two solid rocket boosters to push the orbiter into the sky.

The external fuel tank was the only part of the craft not reused in some way. The solid rocket boosters detached after a few minutes and parachuted into the ocean. Ships collected them so they could be recycled. After the orbiter's mission was complete, it **glided** back to Earth and was prepared for another flight.

NASA engineers had initially planned for space shuttles to make dozens of flights per year. But they averaged less than five per year, even with four orbiters. What happened? In 1986, the space shuttle orbiter Challenger broke apart 73 seconds after liftoff due to a problem with one of its boosters. In the 2003, the orbiter Columbia broke apart during reentry due to damage it had sustained during launch. Each accident killed seven astronauts and spurred lengthy, expensive investigations and redesigns, during which the shuttles were grounded. The operational costs ended up being more than 20 times higher than what was first thought. NASA and government space agencies soured on reusability, opting instead to develop disposable rockets to replace the space shuttle.

Although the space shuttle project was more expensive, less useful, and more dangerous than NASA had originally envisioned, it was not a complete failure. With it, astronauts were able to launch, repair, and upgrade the Hubble Space Telescope, which has provided scientists and the public alike with stunning images of the universe for some 30 years. It ferried parts and astronauts to build the International Space Station (ISS), the largest structure ever built in space.

WHAT MIGHT HAVE BEEN...

As NASA was evaluating ideas for the space shuttle in the 1960's and early 1970's, many different ideas were developed. Some designs were very different from the design that finally won out.

HOW REUSABLE ROCKETS WORK

Reusing a rocket isn't as simple as reusing an airplane. Rocket components (parts) have to be specially designed to resist the wear and tear of multiple launches and atmospheric **reentries.** But the payoff for all that hard engineering work is huge.

Strong components. In traditional rockets, pieces are made as light as possible to save weight. Reusable rocket components are reinforced and made of extra-strong materials. They might be heavier or cost more, but they can survive the punishing conditions of launch, reentry, and landing over and over again.

Grid fins. Ever try balancing a pencil on the tip of your finger? That's similar to the way a reusable **booster** has to balance to land. To make it a bit easier, some reusable rockets use special devices called grid fins to steady themselves as they return to Earth. Grid fins are placed near the top of the booster.

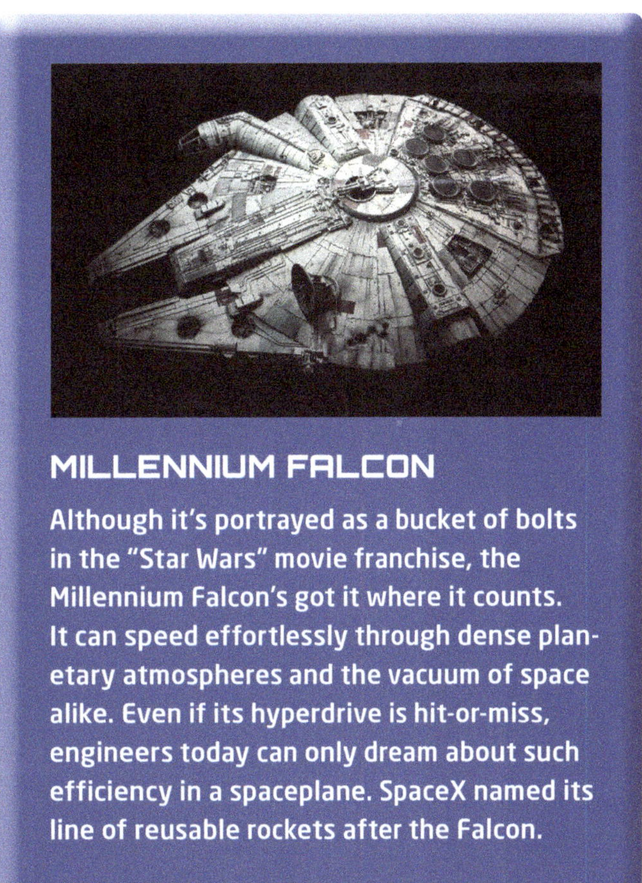

MILLENNIUM FALCON

Although it's portrayed as a bucket of bolts in the "Star Wars" movie franchise, the Millennium Falcon's got it where it counts. It can speed effortlessly through dense planetary atmospheres and the vacuum of space alike. Even if its hyperdrive is hit-or-miss, engineers today can only dream about such efficiency in a spaceplane. SpaceX named its line of reusable rockets after the Falcon.

Landing legs. Reusable rockets feature strong, retractable landing legs. To keep the rocket aerodynamic, they are kept retracted next to the rocket's body until seconds before landing.

Landing pad. A reusable rocket has to land somewhere. For some missions, it can land at a special landing pad not far from the launchpad. For other mission profiles, the rocket can land on a specialized barge at sea.

After landing. After it lands, a reusable booster is brought back to a workshop and thoroughly tested. Parts that don't pass muster are repaired or replaced. Then, the booster is mated to another upper stage and payload and refueled to be launched again.

FLYING HIGHER AND HIGHER

Imagine that you're in a sleek spacecraft, admiring the pitch-blackness of space, the curvature of the horizon, and the splendor of Earth beneath you. Your ship performs a few thruster maneuvers, and you start dropping back down into the atmosphere. After a white-knuckle descent, during which the surface of your craft reaches glowing-hot temperatures, you touch down gently on a runway.

Such a craft is called a spaceplane. Spaceplanes get to orbit in a variety of ways, but they all glide to a landing back on Earth. So each one has to have wings or some other feature that gives them lift in the atmosphere, but that can also survive the rigors of spaceflight.

The most famous spaceplane was the space shuttle orbiter. It had its own engines, but took off vertically with an external fuel tank and boosters that helped get it into orbit. That's one way of approaching the spaceplane challenge, but there are others. Spaceplanes under development today promise cheaper, more convenient access to space.

The Saenger space-plane, illustrated here, is designed to soar high above Earth's atmosphere and launch a detachable shuttle into orbit.

ENGINEERING CHALLENGE: WHAT'S SO HARD ABOUT FLYING TO SPACE?

Airplanes travel at high altitudes. Even commercial airplanes cruise as high as 45,000 feet (13,700 meters), seemingly not that far from the edge of the atmosphere. Why couldn't a pilot just punch the throttle and continue into space?

Engines produce power from the *combustion* (burning) of fuel and **oxygen.** Airplane engines get this oxygen from the atmosphere. But the air thins out higher above Earth, meaning there is less oxygen to feed combustion of engines. The engines of passenger planes don't work much above 50,000 feet (15,000 meters). Specialized jet engines can operate at even higher altitudes and propel a plane to several times the speed of sound. But above 100,000 feet (30,000 meters), there is not enough oxygen to power even the most advanced jet engines.

So regular airplanes can't fly to space. But unlike airplane engines, rocket engines burn their propellant using oxygen supplied from tanks. This allows them to function in space. But can you just strap a rocket engine to a regular airplane? Such a craft would be a single-stage-to-orbit, or SSTO, spaceplane, widely considered the holy grail of reusable rocket technology. Rather than blast off from an isolated launchpad and shed spent stages on the way to orbit, an ideal SSTO spaceplane could take off from a regular

NASA's planned X-33 Reusable Launch Vehicle (RLV), illustrated *(left)* in orbit, and the Skylon spaceplane by Reaction Engines *(illustrated right),* will combine the fuel efficiency of a jet with the power and high speed of a rocket to achieve SSTO flight.

airport (or military airstrip, at least), reach orbit, and return to Earth and land on a regular runway. Such a craft would dramatically bring down the cost of getting to orbit.

But of course, designing such a spaceplane is not easy. A spaceplane has to be a certain shape and made of special materials to withstand the extreme heat and forces felt during reentry into the atmosphere. And those shapes aren't very good for flying at lower altitudes. On top of that, needing more than one type of engine and bringing along oxygen makes a spaceplane even heavier.

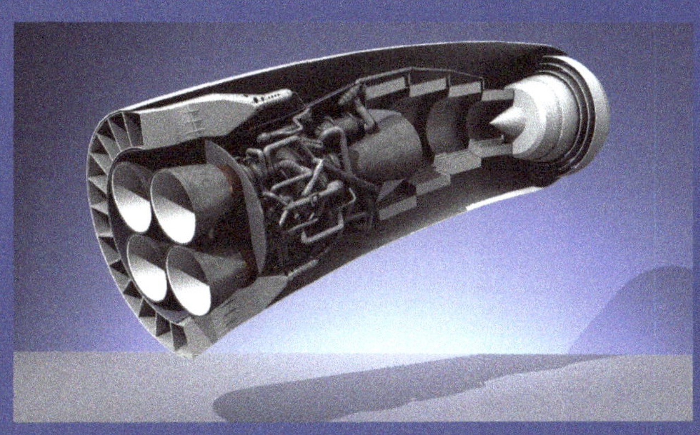

SABRE FOR SSTO—ALPHABET SOUP TO SPACE

The British company Reaction Engines is building a revolutionary new engine that could be the heart of SSTO spaceplanes. This engine, called Synergetic Air-Breathing Rocket Engine (SABRE), can change to accommodate the decreasing air density and increasing speed over the flight. But at the edge of space, the engine can switch to using stored oxygen. If a craft only needs to carry one type of engine and just enough oxygen for the space-based leg of its journey, it could reach space using just a single stage with enough thrust left over to carry payload.

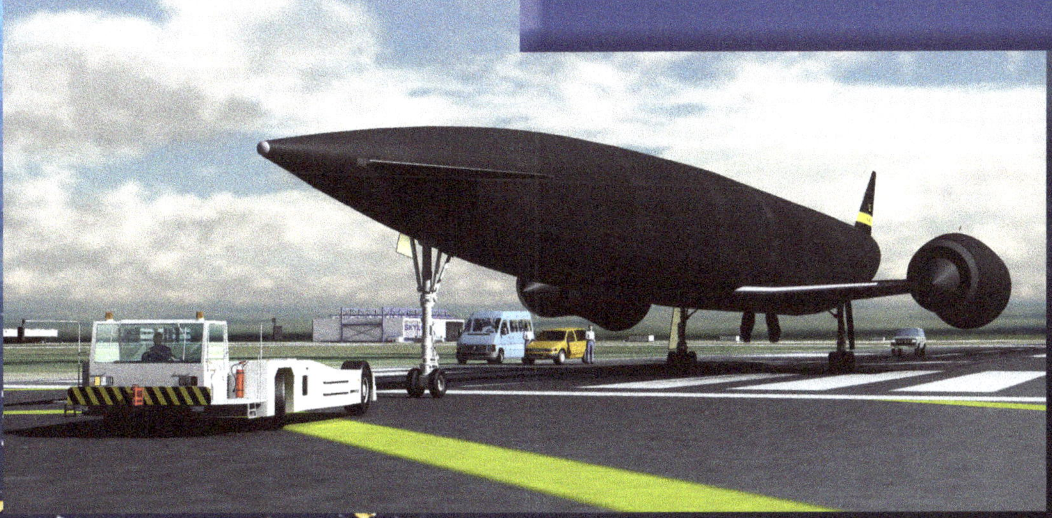

Staging. Getting to space is hard. So far, all spaceplanes have had an earlier stage in the form of a rocket booster or a specialized airplane to help them reach space.

Heat shielding. Spaceplanes have a big surface area compared to the teardrop-shaped capsules usually used to return people from space. As a spaceplane plows through the atmosphere at thousands of miles or kilometers per hour, it compresses the air in front of it. This causes the air to heat up to thousands of degrees. Single-use capsules have a layer of material that burns off to protect the crew inside. But since spaceplanes are meant to be reused, they are instead covered with special tiles that heat up very slowly.

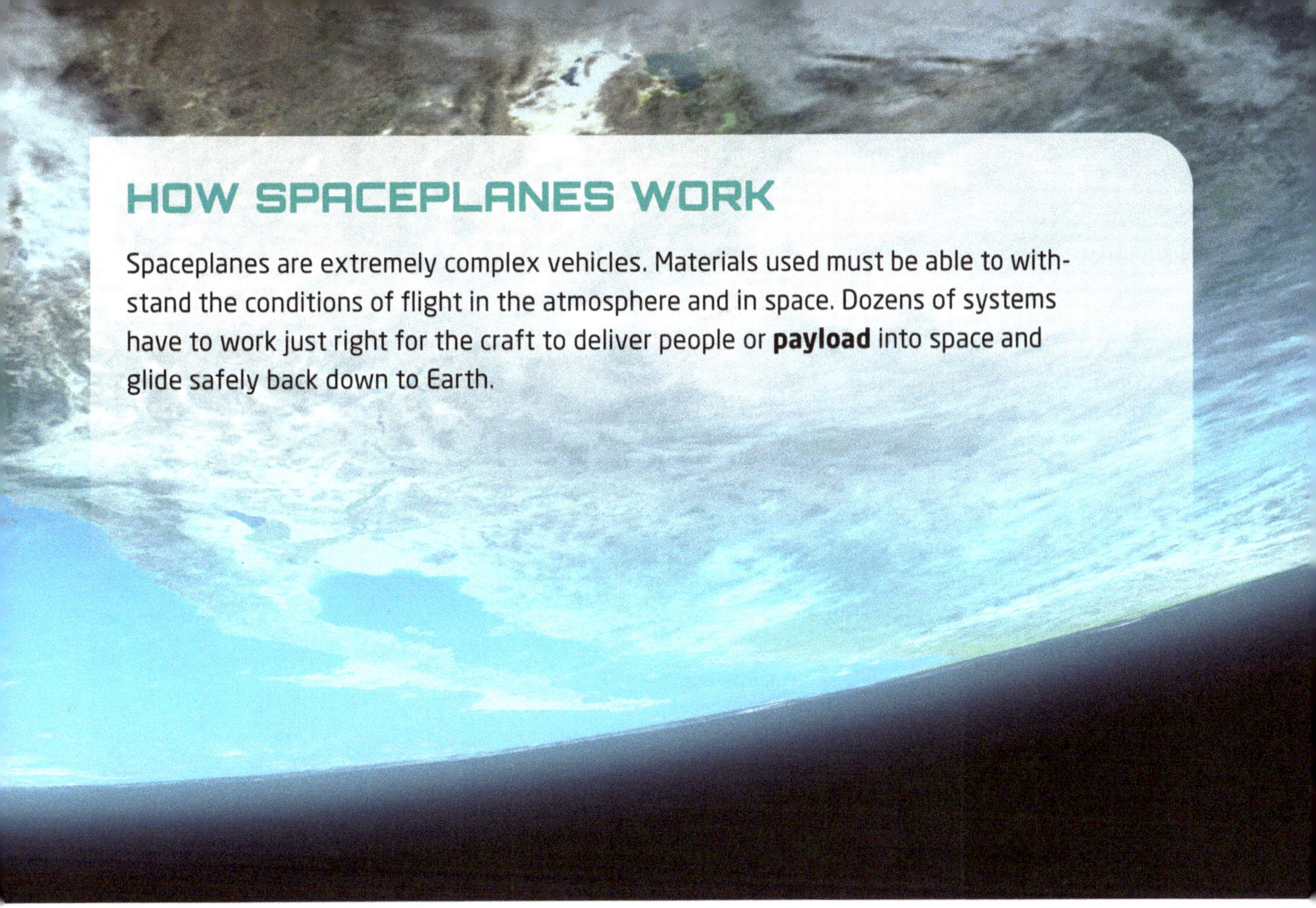

HOW SPACEPLANES WORK

Spaceplanes are extremely complex vehicles. Materials used must be able to withstand the conditions of flight in the atmosphere and in space. Dozens of systems have to work just right for the craft to deliver people or **payload** into space and glide safely back down to Earth.

Engines. A spaceplane can have one or more jet engines or rocket engines. They may even have **hybrid** engines that combine features of the two.

Landing. All spaceplanes glide to a landing. This requires less logistical considerations than having enough fuel left over for a powered landing. Shouldn't they be called "spacegliders," then?

SPACEPLANES OF TODAY AND TOMORROW

Several spaceplanes are seeking to soar out from under the space shuttle's long shadow. Their builders want to fulfill the orbiter's promise of cheap, quick, and reliable access to space.

Dream Chaser. Initially begun as a NASA concept, the Dream Chaser is a spaceplane being developed by American company Sierra Nevada Corporation. The Dream Chaser looks—and will function—a bit like a stubby space shuttle orbiter. It will launch vertically, stowed at the top of a rocket like a satellite. Of course, since it is much smaller than a shuttle orbiter, it can either hold passengers or supplies, but not both, and not as much stuff. It will be able to carry seven people, however, just as many as the space shuttle orbiters. After its mission, it can land **autonomously** on any large runway.

X-37b. It sounds like a conspiracy theory, but it's actually true: the U.S. military has a spaceplane performing mysterious missions in Earth's orbit. The X-37b is a small, uncrewed spaceplane that is launched atop a conventional rocket. It has orbited Earth in several secret missions, each longer than the last. Nobody outside the U.S. military knows what it's doing up there, but experts think it's testing materials and sensors for future spy satellites—and technology for larger future spaceplanes.

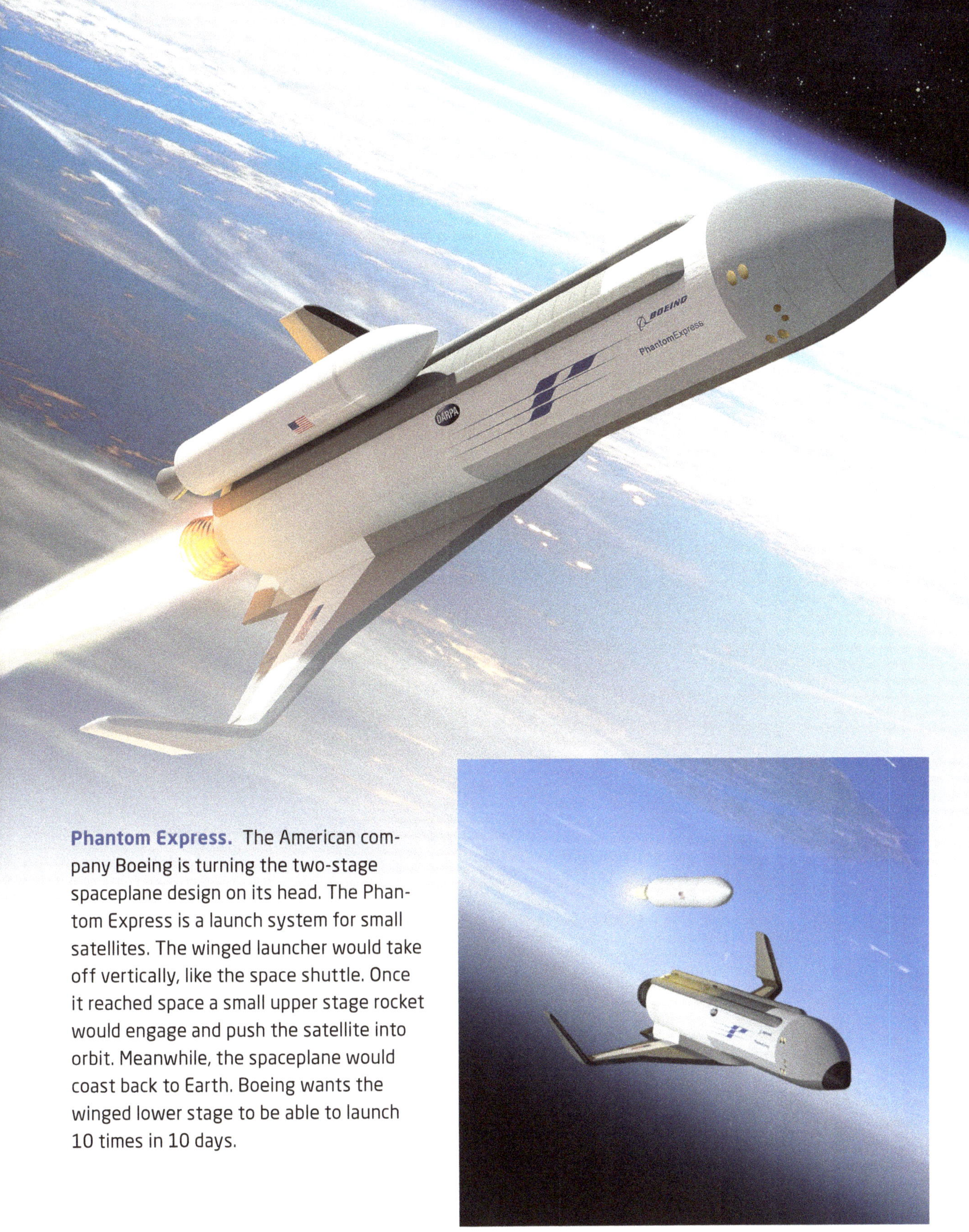

Phantom Express. The American company Boeing is turning the two-stage spaceplane design on its head. The Phantom Express is a launch system for small satellites. The winged launcher would take off vertically, like the space shuttle. Once it reached space a small upper stage rocket would engage and push the satellite into orbit. Meanwhile, the spaceplane would coast back to Earth. Boeing wants the winged lower stage to be able to launch 10 times in 10 days.

3 ROBOTS EXPLORING SPACE

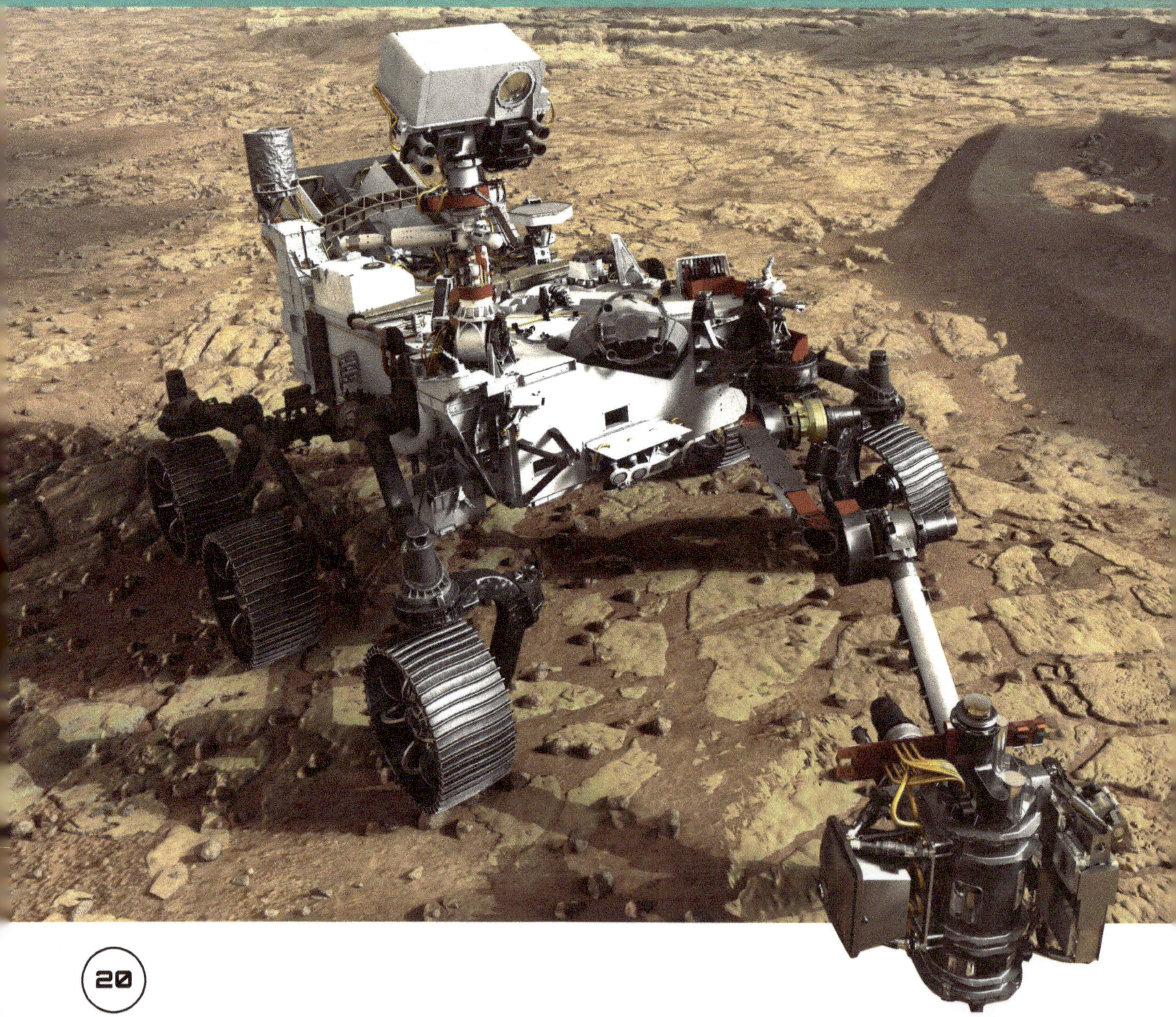

OUR EYES AND EARS—AND GRIPPERS—IN SPACE

Wouldn't it be great to visit Mars? But you'd need food for your journey as well as your stay. And water. And shelter. And air. And a way to get down to the surface without getting flattened. Oh, and a fully fueled, fully stocked spacecraft to get back home.

It's easy to see why we've sent space probes and rovers to explore the solar system. They don't need air, water, or food. Just a power source will do. They can be designed to withstand all kinds of environments that would be deadly for living things. We humans usually want to come back home when we're done exploring! A robot explorer can be left behind when its mission is over. For these reasons, robots have dominated space exploration. Humans have only made it as far as the moon, but probes and rovers explore the distant reaches of our solar system.

But robots can do more than just take our place in space. They can work with people so they can do more in space. Robots already assist astronauts on the International Space Station. Soon, **humanoid** robots might fly to space with astronauts and help them perform routine tasks.

An artist's rendition *(left)* of NASA's proposed Mars 2020 rover, a robotic explorer that will search the Red Planet for habitable conditions where life may have existed in the past and may still exist today.

Canadarm2 is a giant robotic arm on the ISS that repairs and upgrades the station, catches incoming spacecraft, and even moves astronauts around! Canadarm2 doesn't have a fixed position on the ISS. Each end of the arm can be "plugged in" to different slots around the outside of the space station, allowing Canadarm2 to move like a giant Slinky. It also has a 50-foot (15-meter) boom attachment for observing remote parts of the ISS, as well as a hand-like robotic attachment called Dextre.

ROBOTS HELPING ASTRONAUTS

Space exploration isn't either robots or people: it can be "both. . .and." Future space missions will almost certainly combine human and robot missions. Some jobs may require human hands. But robots can also help improve human capability in space.

HELPFUL SPACE 'BOTS

Science fiction is full of robots helping human protagonists. We're not close to copying the general resourcefulness of the "Star Wars " franchise's plucky astromech droids or the sarcastic TARS of *Interstellar.* But they continue to inspire engineers to work towards designing similar robotic helpers.

NASA is also experimenting with robots that can work inside the ISS. In 2011, a robotic astronaut was brought aboard called Robonaut 2, or R2 for short. Although the robot was brought up for testing, it quickly made itself useful, autonomously performing simple experiments and cleaning the station. But R2 was just a torso. NASA, encouraged by initial results, wanted to give it legs for greater mobility. So in 2014, astronauts aboard the ISS performed the world's first surgery on a robot in space. The leg attachment was successful at first, but a nagging wiring problem damaged the robot over time, and it had to be returned to Earth in 2018. Engineers are hoping that R2 or a successor will be returned to the ISS soon.

ROBOTS FLYING SOLO

Much of space is no place for people. Instead, robotic probes, landers, and rovers will explore the solar system for us. Robots can go where it is too dangerous for humans. Robots don't need food, water, or sleep as humans do. They can even explore planet surfaces where there is almost no air!

Curiosity. NASA's car-sized rover Curiosity has explored Mars since 2012. It treks around the surface of Mars collecting information about the area where it landed. Specifically, Curiosity has confirmed that its landing site once held conditions favorable to the development of life. Whether life actually did develop will be up to future missions to figure out...

Hayabusa2. In 2014, Japan launched the Hayabusa2 spacecraft to study the **asteroid** Ryugu. The probe came with a small army of four landers that took advantage of Ryugu's low gravity to bounce around its surface. Hayabusa2 itself collected samples of the asteroid to return to Earth for study.

Future: Exotic engineering for exotic places. Not every planet and moon in the solar system has a rocky, dusty surface. Some have gaseous atmospheres, underground caverns, or even oceans of water or other liquids on their surface or buried beneath miles of rock or ice. Such features are hard to study with traditional landers and rovers. Engineers are designing novel probes to explore these places. For instance, a robot might be made of gears and pulleys to explore the surface of Venus with its high temperatures and crushing pressures, or balloon-like probes might float through the cloud-tops of Jupiter.

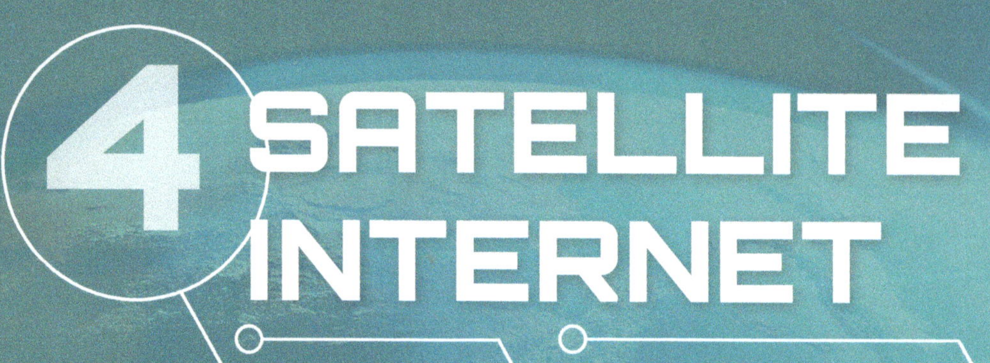

4 SATELLITE INTERNET

A SERIES OF TUBES IN SPACE

Imagine you're exploring a desert, or hiking in a vast national park. Say you get lost or hurt. Cellphone service is nonexistent. What do you do? What if you could pull out a pizza-box-sized receiver and connect in real time to authorities? And you could shop online while you wait to be rescued! That's the promise of satellite internet!

Today, you have three main ways to connect to the internet. You can connect a laptop or desktop computer to a modem with an ethernet cable, or you can use a wireless connection to a **modem** (called Wifi). But both of these methods require that the modem be connected to a cable. You can use a smartphone network, but you need to be within range of cell phone towers to do so.

With satellite internet, all you would need is a receiver and a device with which to use the connection, such as a smartphone or computer to get a blazing-fast connection—anytime, anywhere.

Full satellite internet networks will take thousands of satellites and many years to come online. But in the meantime, even a more modest deployment of satellite internet will be helpful. Embedding sensors into objects can allow people to learn their status. This concept is called the internet of things (IoT). But many things that would be useful to keep track of, such as power lines and ocean buoys, are not near traditional internet connections. Small networks of internet satellites could allow these connected devices to report in a few times a day. The connection doesn't need to be the highest quality or even connected all the time—that agriculture sensor doesn't need to stream movies, it just needs to ping the farmer that the cornfield is getting a bit dry.

GSO NETWORKS VS. LEO NETWORKS

Satellite internet is here already! But. . . you might not want it. It often serves as the network of last resort for people in rural communities or other remote locations. Current satellite networks are slow. But new technologies promise to make satellite internet much faster.

GSO networks. Current satellite internets are far from Earth. Satellite internet that exists today is provided by a few large satellites in geostationary orbit (GSO). This has some advantages. The satellites' geostationary orbits mean they stay fixed in one place relative to the ground and can function as a relatively simple relay from ground to satellite to ground. The great distance from Earth required to reach GSO means that only a few satellites are needed to cover most of Earth's surface. These powerful satellites can handle huge amounts of traffic.

Latency. A great connection with only a few satellites? Why isn't everybody using satellite internet? There's a downside: GSO networks suffer from high latency. Latency is the time it takes information to travel across a network. So low latency is good, and high latency is bad. Information travels faster in space, but it has much farther to go: 22,300 miles (35,900 kilometers) from Earth's surface to the satellite, and the same distance back down. That means it can take up to a half-second to get a response. This is not a problem for streaming shows or music, but it makes surfing the web annoying and playing multiplayer games impossible.

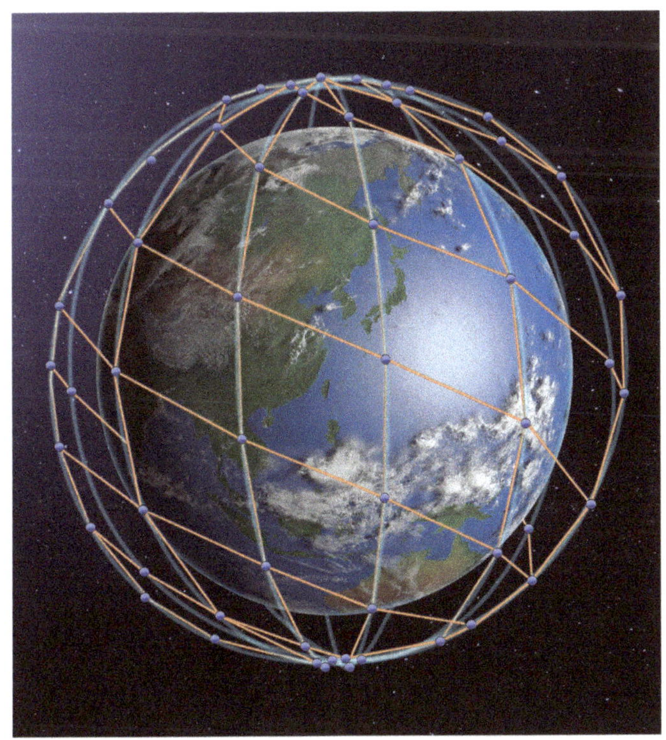

LEO networks. Today, companies designing satellite internet constellations, such as SpaceX and Amazon, are planning to place them in low Earth orbit (LEO). Such satellites will offer very low latency connections, since they will only be hundreds, not thousands, of miles or kilometers above Earth's surface. But many satellites will be needed because each one will only be able to reach a small piece of Earth's surface. Companies that are using this approach are planning on launching hundreds or thousands of satellites. On top of that, satellites in LEO are constantly moving over Earth's surface. LEO satellites will have lasers to transfer traffic from one satellite to another as they travel over a fixed location on Earth. Such networks would offer blistering fast connections anywhere in the world.

5 SPACE TOURISM

LIFTOFF TO ADVENTURE

Have you ever been to space? Probably not! Despite recent advancements in rocket technology, it is still extremely expensive to launch people into space. Fewer than 600 people have gone to space—almost all of them as part of government space programs.

Seven people have gone to space for fun. From 2001 to 2009, the Russian space agency Roscosmos was transporting two cosmonauts at a time to the ISS, but its Soyuz spacecraft could hold three people. So, Roscosmos partnered with American company Space Adventures to train citizens to fly to the ISS and spend a few days there. But the once-in-a-lifetime experience came at an astronomical price. Each space tourist paid tens of millions of dollars for the opportunity.

Soon, many more people may have access to space. Several companies are designing spacecraft specifically for giving tourists brief rides into space. Rather than relying on extra seats on government spacecraft, these craft will seat several people.

Space tourism might help people to better understand our place in the universe. For many astronauts, looking down on Earth brought about a life-changing shift in perspective. This is called the overview effect. Some supporters of space tourism hope that space tourists may focus their attention on such things as protecting the environment and helping other people as a result of the overview effect.

REACHING FOR THE STARS

Soon, many more people are going to join the ranks of space tourists. Several companies are poised to launch paying customers into space. If you can afford it, you can probably book your trip to space right now!

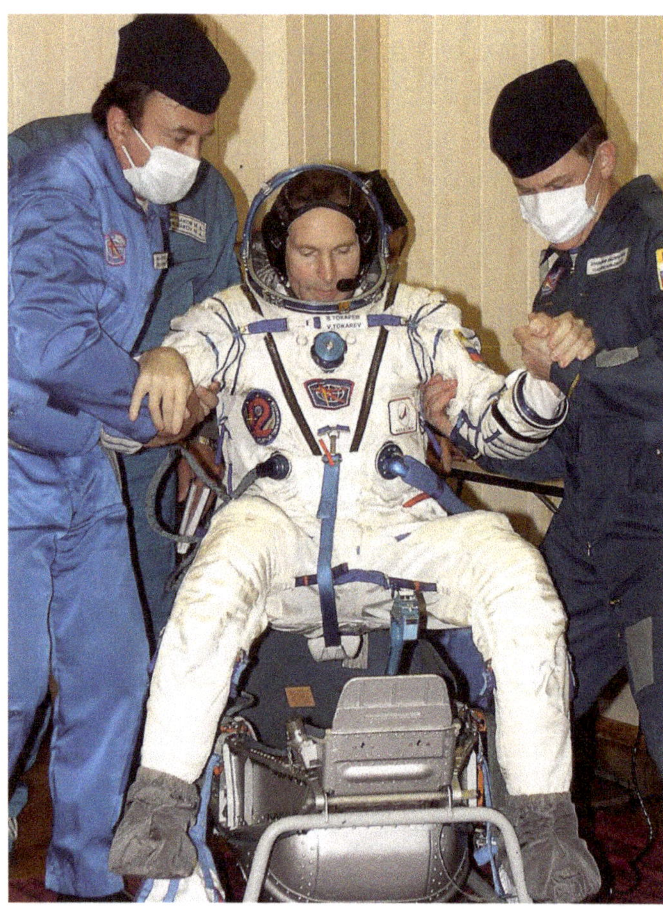

Training. Some companies might require hours, days, or weeks of training. But the amount is likely to be far less than what was required by Space Adventures and Roscosmos, since the tourists will be on spacecraft specially designed for space tourism and will only spend a few hours in space at most.

Virgin Galactic. Virgin Galactic is a space company founded by British businessman Sir Richard Branson. A specially designed airplane called WhiteKnightTwo carries a spaceplane called SpaceShipTwo to an altitude of about 50,000 feet (15,000 meters). Then, SpaceShipTwo rockets six passengers up into **suborbital** space.

SpaceShipTwo tragedy. Space tourism looked like it was poised to take off earlier in the decade. But in 2014, Virgin Galactic's first SpaceShipTwo broke apart during a test flight, killing the copilot and seriously injuring the pilot. The breakup was caused by copilot error, but a U.S. government study found that the design of the spaceplane's controls made it too easy for such mistakes to become deadly. Virgin Galactic spent years building a new SpaceShipTwo with more **failsafe** controls.

SpaceX is planning to use space tourism as a means to an end, not as a business objective itself. In 2018, the company announced that it had reached an agreement with Japanese billionaire Yusaku Maezawa to "rent" the first crewed flight around the moon in its giant Starship, which is currently under development (see page 44-45). Maezawa, an avid art collector, will be inviting several artists of different disciplines to share the experience. Although the terms of the deal were not made public, SpaceX owner Elon Musk *(left)* stated that Maezawa paid "a nontrivial amount" for the honor. The flight around the moon could happen as early as 2023.

Blue Origin is a space company founded by Amazon CEO Jeff Bezos. The company has been testing a rocket for space tourism called the New Shepard. A booster propels a capsule with room for six people into space. The capsule spends a few minutes in space before parachuting back down to the ground. The booster lands separately, and both it and the capsule are reused.

Bigelow Aerospace. The American company Bigelow Aerospace is working on creating space hotels. Rather than relying on dozens of launches or futuristic space construction methods, Bigelow Aerospace is designing inflatable modules. A thick, fabric compartment is packed inside a payload faring. It is filled with air once it reaches space. In 2016, the Bigelow Expandable Activity Module (BEAM) was successfully attached to the ISS and expanded. Today, astronauts report how the BEAM is holding up in space—and use it for storage. It's like a space station shed! Bigelow Aerospace hopes to create a hotel in the next few years that will be the go-to destination for space tourists.

Price. The ticket prices of both Blue Origin and Virgin Galactic are rumored to be around $250,000. That's still incredibly expensive, but far less than what the first seven space tourists paid. Officials from both companies are expecting ticket prices to fall eventually, bringing space within the reach of merely rich people. A stay at a Bigelow Aerospace hotel will probably exceed $10 million.

6 COLONIZING THE SOLAR SYSTEM

Many thinkers believe the future of humanity lies in space. While no human has yet to venture beyond the moon, space technology is rapidly improving. Most agree that humans will achieve interplanetary travel.

MAKING LIFE MULTIPLANETARY

Humans are at home on Earth. But it's not without its problems. Some people are worried that a disaster, such as an asteroid strike or effects of runaway global warming, could wipe out some or all life on Earth. They see it as a duty to colonize other worlds so people—and other life—can survive.

Other people want to colonize space for the money. The solar system contains more valuable resources than we could imagine. If just a tiny fraction outside of Earth could be accessed, the miners could be extremely wealthy.

We want to learn more things about the solar system. But robotic probes and landers can only do so much. People are more flexible and faster than robots. The number of experiments an astronaut could perform in a single day would probably take a rover many months or even years, so sending astronauts to the surface of a solar system body would allow scientists to learn much more about it.

Whatever the reasoning, living away from the friendly confines of Earth is going to be extremely challenging. We've only taken a few baby steps out of our Earthen nursery. Many more engineering challenges lie ahead for us to become a multiplanetary species.

SPACE STATIONS

Apart from Earth, the most convenient place to live is right next to it. Space stations are great places to conduct experiments, test technology, and study the effects of weightlessness on people and other living things.

Mir. The space station Mir was the first space station where people spent significant time away from Earth. The Soviet Union, a former country once made up of Russia and several other territories to its west and southwest, began its construction in 1986. It was much larger than the experimental temporary space stations that had come before it, but it was still cramped and dangerous. Mir orbited Earth for 15 years before it was abandoned and allowed to crash into the Pacific Ocean.

Chinese space station. While other countries have cooperated on the International Space Station (see pages 40-41), China has gone it alone. It tested two temporary space stations in the 2010's. It plans to begin construction of a permanent space station, about the size of Mir, in 2020.

Not much there. Space stations don't have lots of potential to become large colonies. Aside from the (important) experimentation done at space stations, there isn't much more a floating space colony could offer, apart from exotic weightless manufacturing processes and relatively easy access to Earth.

THE INTERNATIONAL SPACE STATION

The only permanent **colony** off Earth's surface orbits some 250 miles (400 kilometers) above us. The International Space Station (ISS) is an orbital outpost for research and experimentation.

The United States and Russia have long been rivals. But in the 1990's, conditions allowed them to collaborate on the ISS. The Cold War, an intense, 55-year rivalry between the U.S. and the Soviet Union, had just ended with the Soviet Union's collapse. Both sides had been looking to build new space stations. But budgets for the projects were spiraling out of control. So in 1993, the U.S. and Russia, the largest former member state of the Soviet Union, agreed to build a single space station together. They sought input and help from other countries as well. Thus, the International Space Station was born.

The ISS is the single most expensive object ever built, costing more than $100 billion. It has been the site of countless experiments, educational videos, and even the first space tourists (see pages 30-31)! It has been continuously crewed by at least three astronauts or cosmonauts for almost 20 years.

The ISS has also been the site of many experiments involving extended stays in space. From 2015 to 2016, U.S. astronaut Scott Kelly and the Russian cosmonaut Mikhail Kornienko took part in a one-year mission to examine the health effects of spending long periods in space aboard the ISS. Kelly's identical twin brother, the retired NASA astronaut Mark Kelly, also took part in the study. Over the course of the mission and after Scott's return from space, doctors evaluated and compared the brothers' health. During Kelly and Kornienko's time there, they sampled lettuce grown in the ISS. Such experiments are intended to help make future missions more sustainable—as well as to increase the variety in the astronauts' diets.

Despite only being completed in 2011, the ISS is old. Some of its parts have been in space for more than twenty years. Only funded until 2024, it faces an unclear future. Some experts want to continue updating and using the ISS, while others feel it will no longer be useful. Still others want to give more access to private companies. To complicate matters, tensions between the U.S. and Russia are high again. Russia even floated the idea of removing its modules to make its own separate space station.

HOW SPACE COLONIES WILL WORK

No one envisioned Earth's orbit being the final destination of space exploration. Orbital flights and space stations have always been seen as the stepping stones to bigger things, such as visits and permanent colonies on other bodies in the solar system.

Profit. Space colonies will be incredibly expensive. They are not likely to be created just for fun. It's possible that some colonies might be created by rich people who just want to get away from it all. But for the most part, a colony will have to make money. Perhaps the best way is through mining. Other bodies possess nearly limitless amounts of valuable resources. If their value exceeds the cost of bringing them back to Earth, then mining them might be worth it. Other resources might be worth more where they are mined. For instance, if an asteroid colony could extract resources to make rocket fuel, it could become a gas station in space. Spacecraft from Earth could travel there to refuel before traveling farther out into the solar system.

Protection. The sun puts out harmful **radiation.** Earth's ozone layer protects us from most of it. But in space and on some planets, there is no such protection. Engineers will have to come up ways to protect space colonists from this harmful radiation. Some ideas include burying colonies underground or housing them in caves, since harmful radiation cannot pass through rock. These habitations would also be easier to keep at a comfortable temperature. People might even be able to fill them with air, so colonists wouldn't have to wear spacesuits.

Sustainability. Whatever the purpose of a space colony, it will have to sustain itself somehow. Transport to and from Earth would be infrequent, so colonists would likely have to grow much of their own food and make their own power. 3D printing technologies will help them create some of the items they need to sustain and grow the colony.

COLONY CONCEPTS

Other than near-Earth space stations, colonizing space is probably a long way off.
The financial and technological hurdles will be unlike any encountered before.
But that hasn't stopped people from dreaming.

SpaceX Starship. Elon Musk founded SpaceX in 2002 with the goal of colonizing Mars. Now that his company has achieved reusability with the Falcon 9, it has begun work on the booster and spacecraft that Musk hopes will eventually allow people to colonize Mars. The Starship could carry dozens of people to the surface of Mars. The Super Heavy booster would launch Starships, refueling tankers, and cargo vessels into orbit around Earth. Musk envisions sending cargo missions first, perhaps with robots to help prepare the site, followed on shortly by Starships full of colonists. He wants to charge people $200,000 for a one-way ticket to Mars.

The sky was the limit. After the rapid advances in spaceflight in the 1960's, experts thought space colonies were only a few decades away. NASA itself commissioned elaborate illustrations of people relaxing in giant space **habitats.** But it was not meant to be. NASA's post-Apollo budget was slashed and many people lost interest in space travel.

GLOSSARY

asteroid a rocky or metallic object smaller than a planet that orbits a star.

atmosphere the mass of gases that surrounds a planet or other heavenly body.

autonomous capable of acting independently.

booster any one of various devices for increasing the power or thrust of an engine.

colony a territory distant from the country that governs it.

engineer a professional who plans and builds engines, machines, roads, or the like.

failsafe some feature for automatically counteracting the effect of a possible source of failure.

glide to come down slowly, as with an airplane, without using an engine or motor.

habitat a place of dwelling.

humanoid having human characteristics or form.

hybrid combining two or more functions or modes of operation.

modem a device used in telecommunications.

orbit the path of an artificial satellite or spacecraft around any celestial body.

oxygen a gaseous chemical element that makes up a portion of the air.

payload the load carried by an aircraft, train, truck, or other vehicle.

radiation energy given off in the form of waves or tiny particles of matter.

reentry the return of a rocket or spacecraft into the Earth's atmosphere after flight into space.

suborbital below the altitude necessary to achieve orbit around the Earth.

INDEX

ACKNOWLEDGMENTS

5 NASA/KSC

6-7 NASA/Joel Kowsky; © Joe Raedle, Getty Images

8-9 NASA/JSC; NASA/Terry Zaperach; National Archives

10-11 SpaceX; © Manfred Schmid, Getty Images

12-13 © Detlev Van Ravenswaay, Science Photo Library

14-15 © IMp Photo/Shutterstock; NASA/J. Frassanito & Associates; © BAE Systems; © Reaction Engines

16-17 © Virgin Galactic; © Travel View/Shutterstock; © Frederic J. Brown, AFP/Getty Images; © Steve Mann, Shutterstock

18-19 U.S. Air Force; NASA/Ken Ulbrich; NASA/Boeing; DARPA

20-21 NASA/JPL-Caltech

22-23 NASA/JSC; © TY Lim, Shutterstock; NASA

24-25 NASA/JPL-Caltech/MSSS; NASA/JPL-Caltech; Akihiro Ikeshita/JAXA/ESO

26-27 © Oleksiy Maksymenko Photography/Alamy Images

28-29 © Junpinzon/Shutterstock; © Facebook; © LeoSat

30-31 © Daniel Berehulak, Getty Images

32-33 © Sovfoto/UIG/Getty Images; © Tim Ockenden, PA Images/Getty Images; © Virgin Galactic; © Robyn Beck, AFP/Getty Images

34-35 NASA/KSC; © Matthew Staver, Bloomberg/Getty Images; © John B. Carnett, Bonnier Corporation/Getty Images; NASA/JSC

36-37 © Gorodenkoff/Shutterstock; SpaceX

38-39 NASA; © China Academy of Space Technology; NASA/JSC

40-41 NASA

42-43 © E71lena/Shutterstock; NASA

44-45 SpaceX; NASA; NASA Ames Research Center/Rick Guidice

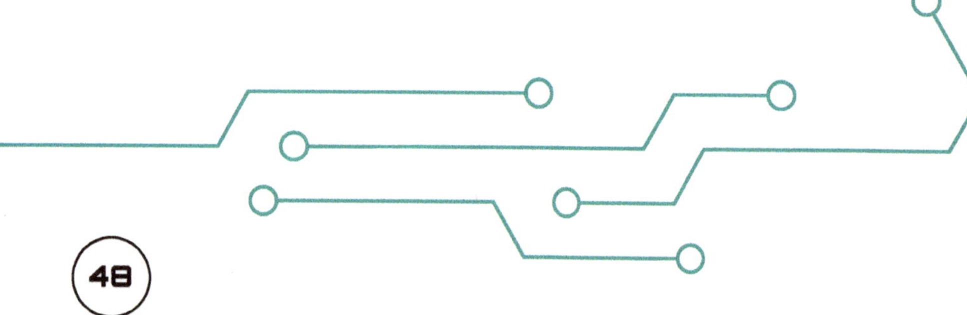